REAL ESTATE EXAM PREP

COLORADO

AF704239

Dearborn™
Real Estate Education

While a great deal of care has been taken to provide accurate and current information, the ideas, suggestions, general principles, and conclusions presented in this text are subject to local, state and federal laws and regulations, court cases, and any revisions of same. The reader is urged to consult legal counsel regarding any points of law. This publication should not be used as a substitute for competent legal advice.

Publisher: Evan M. Butterfield
Senior Development Editor: Kristen Short
Development Editor: Amanda Rahn
Associate Development Editor: Michael J. Scafuri
Senior Managing Editor: Ronald J. Liszkowski
Art Manager: Lucy Jenkins
Cover Design: Gail Chandler

Testbank Reviewer: John K. Stovall
Exam Prep Series Content Consultant: Marie Spodek, DREI

Copyright 2001 by Dearborn™ Real Estate Education, a division of Dearborn Financial Publishing, Inc.®

Published by Dearborn™ Real Estate Education
a division of Dearborn Financial Publishing, Inc.®
155 North Wacker Drive
Chicago, IL 60606-1719
http://www.dearbornRE.com

All rights reserved. The text of this publication, or any part thereof, may not be reproduced in any manner whatsoever without written permission from the publisher.

Printed in the United States of America.

01 02 03 10 9 8 7 6 5 4 3 2 1

Introduction

Welcome to *Colorado Exam Prep*! When you bought this book, you showed that you are serious about passing the exam and getting your real estate license. This is *NOT* an easy test. For people whose test-taking skills are weak, or who haven't adequately prepared, the exam can be a nightmare. For those who have taken the time and effort to study and review, however, the exam can be a much more positive experience.

It's pretty obvious, though, that if you practice and review key material, your test score will improve. This book is your key to exam success.

The process is simple: Just work your way through the practice questions, taking your time and answering each one carefully. Then check your answers by studying the Answer Key, where you'll find both the correct answer to each question as well as an explanation of *why* that answer is correct. It might be a good idea to review your classroom materials and textbook before you start.

Remember: These 200 questions reflect as closely as possible the topic coverage of the state-specific portion of your exam only! For the balance of the test, you'll need to use a "national" exam prep book. And remember, too, that it takes study and hard work on your part to pass the licensing exam: no single study aid will do the trick alone.

Experts who are familiar with the Colorado licensing examination, as well as real estate law and practice, prepared this book. You've taken the first step toward your success as a real estate professional: Good Luck!

Dearborn Real Estate Education

Introduction

1. Who of the following is exempt from real estate license law?

   A. Attorney at law collecting a five percent commission for helping market a property
   B. Inactive licensee assisting a friend in filling out a purchase offer
   C. Investor who owns 12 investment properties and sells one to an owner-occupant
   D. Right-of-way specialist accepting a commission referral for finding investment acreage for a friend

2. The purpose of the Colorado Real Estate Commission is to

   A. assure that licensees collect only the appropriate commissions.
   B. provide mediation in disputes between brokers and the public.
   C. provide legal assistance to the public regarding real estate transactions.
   D. protect the public of the state of Colorado in real estate matters.

3. If a broker is accused of a violation of license law in a complaint to the commission and the commission investigative staff determines that the violation probably happened, the commission

   A. will hold a public hearing, get evidence, and decide on appropriate penalties.
   B. may decide to refer the matter to a hearing before an appointed administrative law judge.
   C. may suspend the broker's license and levy a fine not to exceed $2,500.
   D. will determine damages, if any, and seek compensation for the party harmed by the broker.

4. The real estate commission must investigate

   A. any verified written complaint.
   B. any licensee accused of a crime.
   C. at least five percent of all brokers each year.
   D. disputes between brokers regarding commission splits.

5. In order to be the broker of record for a corporation, a person must hold

   A. more than a nominal ownership in the corporation.
   B. an executive position as president or chief executive officer.
   C. a valid active Colorado broker's license.
   D. a position as a director with voting rights.

6. In the event that the employing broker of a corporate brokerage is suddenly unable to continue in that position, the commission may issue a temporary "hardship" license to any

   A. member of the board of directors.
   B. Colorado licensee approved by the corporate board of directors.
   C. officer or director with a broker's license from another state.
   D. person who has a sufficient ownership interest in the corporation.

7. When an employing broker changes the primary business address,

   A. all of the licenses of employed licensees must be sent to the commission for reissue at the correct address.
   B. this change will be noted at the next license renewal cycle.
   C. each employed licensee must notify the commission of the change.
   D. the broker must notify the commission in a manner acceptable to the commission, or the brokerage license will become inactive.

8. When must Colorado licenses be renewed?

   A. Each year at the anniversary of licensing
   B. Every three years with expiration on December 31 of the third year
   C. Every three years on the anniversary of licensing
   D. Every three years if the licensee passes the state examination

9. Errors and omissions professional liability insurance is required for

   A. every active Colorado licensee.
   B. active and inactive Colorado licensees.
   C. the employing broker only.
   D. resident Colorado brokers only.

10. In order to renew an active Colorado real estate license, the licensee must complete

    A. 8 hours of mandatory continuing education within the last three years.
    B. 24 hours of continuing education plus successful completion of the Colorado portion of the state licensing examination.
    C. 24 hours of approved continuing education or successful completion of the Colorado portion of the state licensing examination.
    D. 24 hours of additional education from any source.

11. A person maintaining an inactive Colorado real estate license

    A. must complete the usual continuing education and pay the renewal fees when due.
    B. may perform no more than five brokerage activities in any one year.
    C. must complete continuing education for the current renewal cycle before activating the license.
    D. must maintain errors and omissions insurance at all times.

12. Which of the following is authorized for an independent broker under Colorado law?

    A. May only work independently, not in the employ of another broker
    B. May work in the employ of another broker, work independently, or hire and supervise no more than five other licensees
    C. May work independently without the supervision of another broker
    D. May act as a broker for a corporate brokerage as long as there is a qualified employing broker available for supervision and training of associated licensees

13. A brokerage, XYZ Realty, is part of a franchise or marketing cooperative with a strong public image. The broker's advertising must indicate this relationship by advertising
    A. the franchise name with the broker's phone number so that people are led to the correct office.
    B. both the franchise name and XYZ Realty with the same level of prominence.
    C. only XYZ since that is how the license is held with the commission.
    D. the franchise name prominently with "fine print" identifying XYZ.

14. Salesperson J-H paid the local telephone company to list her name in the directory under the real estate heading as "J-H, Real Estate Salesperson, Residential Property My Specialty." Based on this information, J-H must also include
    A. her license number.
    B. the expiration date of her license.
    C. her street address.
    D. the name of her employing broker.

15. A broker has developed a Web site advertising the broker's office. What, if anything, does the broker need to include?
    A. Name and address of the home office and states in which the brokerage holds licenses
    B. License number of the brokerage and a list of current active licensees
    C. Names of active licensees, addresses, and phone numbers
    D. There is no need for any additional disclosures.

16. An associate broker has developed an Internet Web site. What, if anything, must he or she include?
    A. Name and location of the brokerage company that holds the associate's license
    B. Name of the home office of the company that holds the salesperson's license and a list of states in which company is licensed
    C. Names of all licensees in the broker's office and the states in which they are licensed
    D. There is no need for additional disclosures.

17. Listings based on a "net price" are
    A. more profitable because no minimum is set on the amount of commission collectible.
    B. legal in Colorado as long as the seller agrees.
    C. illegal in Colorado at any time.
    D. permissible with approval of the commission.

18. In Colorado, real estate commissions are
    A. set by law.
    B. set by the Colorado Real Estate Commission.
    C. determined by local groups of brokers.
    D. negotiable between the broker and the seller or buyer.

19. Commissions earned by a broker in a real estate sales transaction
    A. are determined by agreement of the broker and his or her principal.
    B. may be shared with an unlicensed person, provided that such person aided the broker in bringing the buyer and seller together.
    C. may be deducted from the earnest money deposit and claimed by the broker as soon as the buyer and seller execute the purchase and sales agreement.
    D. are based on a schedule of commission rates set by the real estate commission.

20. All earnest money received by a broker on behalf of his or her principal must be deposited in an escrow or trust account within
    A. three days of receiving the offer.
    B. three days of obtaining all signatures for the contract.
    C. one business day after the broker learns of acceptance of the offer.
    D. five banking days of receiving all signatures.

21. A broker received an earnest money deposit from a buyer. Under Colorado law, the broker should
    A. open a special, separate escrow account that will contain funds for this transaction only, separate from funds received in any other transaction.
    B. deposit the money in an existing, special non-interest-bearing escrow account in which all earnest money received from buyers may be held at the same time.
    C. immediately deposit the earnest money in the broker's personal interest-bearing checking or savings account.
    D. hold the earnest money deposit in a secure place in the broker's real estate brokerage office until the offer is accepted.

22. Broker B received a buyer's earnest money check for $5,000 and immediately cashed it. At closing, the broker handed the seller a personal check drawn on the broker's own bank account for $5,300, representing the original earnest money plus six percent interest. The broker
    A. should have deposited the money in a special non-interest-bearing bank account.
    B. properly cashed the check but should have kept the interest.
    C. should have deposited the money in his personal bank account and would have been entitled to keep the interest as a service fee.
    D. should have deposited the money in a bank escrow or trust account and should have discussed the interest with the parties.

23. If a broker establishes an account to hold money belonging to others, which of the following is correct?

    A. All checks, deposit slips, and bank statements must include the word "escrow" or "trust" as part of the account name.
    B. The names of all authorized signers must be on the checks.
    C. The account cannot be in the same bank as the broker's personal checking account.
    D. An individual account is required for each transaction.

24. A broker manages three properties for the same owner. One property is in need of emergency repairs, but that owner does not have enough money in the management account to cover the cost. The broker uses excess funds from the account for the emergency then replaces the funds later with a check from the owner. Which of the following is true?

    A. The broker has acted properly by safeguarding the client's interest.
    B. Such action is proper when the management account balance is sufficient.
    C. The broker is in violation of regulations for improperly handling escrow funds.
    D. The broker must use personal funds for repairs if there is not enough money in the management account.

25. A seller listed his house for sale with a broker on February 1. The listing agreement was to last five months. In April, the seller decided that the house was no longer for sale. Which of the following statements is true?

    A. The seller has canceled the agreement, and there are no penalties.
    B. The seller has withdrawn the broker's authority to sell the property and may be subject to reimbursing some broker expenses.
    C. The seller is required by law to leave his house on the market until June.
    D. The real estate commission will decide if the seller's action is justifiable.

26. A Colorado real estate associate broker may lawfully collect compensation from

    A. either a buyer or a seller.
    B. his or her employing broker only.
    C. any party to the transaction or the party's representative.
    D. a licensed real estate broker only.

27. What are the procedures that a salesperson must follow when the salesperson decides to terminate his or her affiliation with the employing broker?

    A. Give the broker an official letter of termination that he or she can send to the real estate commission
    B. Return all customer cards to the employing broker
    C. Return his or her license, along with a letter of termination, to the real estate commission
    D. The salesperson or associate broker has a joint responsibility with the employing broker to assure that the commission is notified.

28. A licensed salesperson or associate broker may hold a concurrent license with more than one employing broker under which of the following circumstances?
    A. Under no circumstances
    B. With the permission of his or her sales manager
    C. With the written consent of the brokers being represented
    D. With the permission of the real estate commission

29. Several weeks after a closing, an associate broker received a thank you letter and a nice bonus check from the seller of the house. The associate broker cashed the check because he felt it was earned. In this situation, which of the following is true?
    A. The associate broker may accept the bonus because he is licensed as an associate broker.
    B. The broker is allowed to accept money if more than 30 days have elapsed since the closing.
    C. The associate broker may accept the money if his broker permits him to do so.
    D. It is a violation of commission regulations to accept the money.

30. When a sole proprietor has his or her license suspended for two years, what effect does this have on the associate brokers and salespeople affiliated with the proprietor?
    A. Affiliates' licenses will be revoked, subject to reinstatement after one year.
    B. Affiliates' licenses will be also be suspended for a two-year period.
    C. Suspension has no effect on the affiliates' licenses.
    D. Affiliates' licenses are inactive until the affiliates are hired by a new employing broker.

31. How long must an independent broker retain transaction records?
    A. Independent brokers who work alone are not required to retain records.
    B. Transaction records must be kept until the transaction is closed.
    C. Transaction records must be maintained for a minimum of four years.
    D. Independent brokers submit records to the real estate commission for safekeeping.

32. In Colorado license law, the terms "employing broker" and "employed licensee" mean that
    A. the employing broker has specific supervisory requirements for all employed licensees.
    B. employed licensees cannot be independent contractors under the rules of the Internal Revenue Service.
    C. employed licensees must be offered a minimum salary and benefits.
    D. supervisory duties of brokers apply only to employees and not to associate brokers who are independent contractors.

33. When is it acceptable for a broker to pay a referral fee to an unlicensed person?

A. It is never acceptable. Only licensed brokers may receive referral fees.
B. It is acceptable if the unlicensed person only helps to identify and qualify one party to the transaction.
C. It is acceptable as long as the unlicensed person does nothing that requires a real estate license.
D. It is acceptable only if the unlicensed person is a party to the transaction.

34. May a broker accept a referral fee from a mortgage lender or mortgage broker?

A. Yes, this practice is a good way to enhance the licensee's income.
B. No, it is never permissible to accept such a fee.
C. Yes, but only if the broker will not be receiving a commission for the same transaction
D. Yes, but only with the permission of the broker's principal or if the broker is not receiving a commission from the same transaction

35. May a broker accept a referral fee from a title insurance company or representative?

A. Yes, this practice is a good way to enhance your income.
B. No, it is never permissible to accept such a fee.
C. Yes, but only if the broker will not be receiving a commission for the same transaction
D. Yes, but only with the permission of the broker's principal or if the broker is not receiving a commission from the same transaction

36. When must a listing broker disclose to the buyer the broker's working relationship with the seller?

A. In writing at the time the contract to buy and sell is signed
B. Orally before writing the contract and in writing before closing
C. In writing before any conversation or discussion
D. In writing before providing specific real estate services

37. If a buyer's agent approaches a for sale by owner, when must the agent disclose the agency relationship?

A. Orally at the first contact and in writing at the first physical meeting
B. When taking the one-party listing on the property
C. Orally unless the buyer wants to submit an offer, then in writing with the offer
D. Disclosure is unnecessary, because the sellers chose to represent themselves.

38. The licensee has an Exclusive-Right-to-Sell listing with a seller as a transaction-broker. When a potential buyer calls on this listing, the licensee must disclose

A. nothing, since state law makes the licensee the buyer's transaction-broker by default.
B. in writing that the licensee represents the seller exclusively and that the buyer will have no working relationship with the licensee's company.
C. in writing that the licensee works with the seller as a transaction-broker and will owe the same duties to the buyer in a purchase transaction.
D. nothing until the potential buyer has seen the property.

39. A licensee listed a home for some sellers as a seller's agent, and it is now under contract. The sellers ask their agent to work with them to find a new home to purchase. In the purchase transaction, the licensee

A. will continue to be their agent for all transactions with them.
B. will be agent for the seller of their next home and must disclose that.
C. does not have to decide until they decide what home they want.
D. may be either an agent or transaction-broker depending on the mutual agreement.

40. A licensee is working with a buyer in a transaction on another broker's listing. What must the licensee do with the personal check the buyers give as an earnest money deposit?

A. Protect it in a safe place until the licensee learns if the offer was accepted
B. Make a copy for the licensee's broker and turn it over to the listing broker
C. Deposit it in licensee's broker's escrow account until closing
D. Wait until the offer is accepted, then turn it over to licensee's broker for deposit

41. An associate broker wants to purchase a property for investment. The property is not listed with any broker. The associate broker must

A. list the property so that he or she can get a commission on the purchase.
B. have his or her broker list the property so that the commission can be properly handled.
C. use a special sales agreement drawn up by a neutral attorney.
D. disclose to the seller that he or she has a license and inform his or her broker of the transaction.

42. A broker's office must

A. be "open to the public" during normal business hours.
B. be a virtual office doing business by phone and using a post office box mailing address.
C. have a physical address where the commission staff can inspect records.
D. be in a commercial office building to comply with zoning.

43. Regarding filling in blanks in a standard commission-approved form, this

A. is the practice of law and must be done by attorneys.
B. is not the practice of law.
C. must be done entirely with preapproved standard clauses.
D. is the practice of law but is specifically permitted by Colorado law.

44. All of the following relationships are acceptable for one brokerage company in a single transaction EXCEPT

A. agent for the buyer and transaction-broker for the seller.
B. agent for the seller with a buyer as an unrepresented customer.
C. dual agent for both buyer and seller.
D. exclusive transaction-broker for the seller and disclosed transaction-broker for the buyer.

45. Which of the following would an unlicensed personal assistant be permitted to do?

A. Show a property to a potential buyer when the licensed associate is busy
B. Complete the contract forms after the licensed associate gets the important things like price and closing date
C. Complete a comparative market analysis for presentation by the licensed associate
D. Host an open house while the licensed associate is showing another listing

46. Unlicensed personal assistants may

A. drive potential buyers to a listing and let them view it by themselves.
B. distribute factual literature prepared by a licensed associate.
C. answer questions about seller's motivations as long as they are correct.
D. complete and present a comparative market analysis.

47. A listing agent receives two similar offers to purchase and sets an appointment with the sellers to present the offers. Another offer comes in from an associate in the same company. In this situation, the licensee should present

A. all three offers for simultaneous review.
B. the in-company offer first as a courtesy to the fellow associate. If it is not accepted, present the other two offers.
C. the older offers first since that is why the appointment was made. If neither is accepted, present the in-company offer at this appointment.
D. the offers in order and ask for a decision on each before moving on to the next.

48. The licensee has an Exclusive-Right-to-Sell agency agreement with the seller plus a Dual Agency Addendum to deal with any in-company transactions. A buyer working with a transaction-broker from another company wants to see this listing. The licensee's relationship in this transaction would be as a(n)

A. agent for the seller.
B. dual agent for both seller and buyer.
C. transaction-broker for the seller, since there can't be agency for one party and transaction-broker for the other.
D. agent for the seller and transaction-broker for the buyer.

49. As the buyer's agent is filling out a Contract to Buy and Sell, the agent asks the young married buyers how they want to take title. The buyers are not sure. The buyer's agent should

A. advise them to take title as joint tenants since that is appropriate for a married couple.
B. leave the choice blank since the title insurance company will know what to do.
C. leave the choice blank and advise the couple to seek legal counsel and inform the agent of their choice later.
D. explain the differences in the various modes and suggest the one that the licensee knows to be correct.

50. Another associate in your office has an agency listing with a Transaction-Broker Addendum. A buyer calls while you are on phone duty. You describe the other associate's listing and agree to meet the buyer there to view it. When the buyer arrives, you should

A. show the listing. The relationship will automatically be transaction-broker, and disclosure is not required.
B. disclose that your brokerage is transaction-broker and get the buyer's signature on the required form. You may not show the property without the signature.
C. disclose the brokerage relationship in writing. If they decline to sign the disclosure, annotate the form and go on to show the property.
D. disclose the brokerage relationship orally. No written disclosure is required since transaction-broker is the default relationship.

51. A licensee has an agency listing. An associate in a branch office is agent for an interested buyer. Neither agent got an addendum signed with their agency agreements. If this buyer tours the agency listing,

A. the broker is an undisclosed dual agent—an illegal relationship.
B. the listing agent must get the addendum signed by both parties before closing.
C. both agents automatically become transaction-brokers by law.
D. There is no problem because both agents are from different offices.

52. What legal duties does a seller's agent owe to an unrepresented buyer?

A. Loyalty, fidelity, and disclosure of material facts about the property
B. No specific duties—agency duties are to the principal
C. Fair and honest dealing and disclosure of material facts about the property
D. Honest dealing and full disclosure of anything the broker knows about the transaction

53. A seller has no knowledge of any plumbing system problems on the property she is selling. In actuality, however, the pipes are seriously corroded and will need to be replaced soon. In the Seller's Property Disclosure, when responding to whether the seller has any knowledge of plumbing system problems, she should respond

A. "yes."
B. "no."
C. "unknown."
D. The seller would not be required to respond to this question.

54. Five years ago, Unit 5B in a condominium community was the site of a brutal and highly publicized murder. The unit was sold to an elderly woman who contracted the AIDS virus in a blood transfusion and died in the unit last year. As the agent for the woman's estate, what are your disclosure responsibilities to prospective purchasers of Unit 5B?

A. You must disclose both the murder and the AIDS-related death.
B. You are specifically prohibited by law from disclosing either event.
C. You are specifically relieved of liability for nondisclosure of either by the Colorado stigmatized property disclosure law.
D. You do not need to disclose the murder, but you must disclose the AIDS-related death.

55. In Colorado, a developer must register with the real estate commission for which of the following projects?

A. Mini-warehouse project with over one hundred storage units
B. Condominium office park with 40 office warehouse units for sale
C. Subdivision of 100 acres into 10 sites for residential use
D. Conversion of an apartment complex into 25 residential condominiums

56. A private owner of a single 20-acre parcel of land wishes to sell off ten acres and retain ten acres for her own use. Which statement is true for this owner?

A. As the private owner, there are no restrictions or registration requirements.
B. The owner is not required to register with the real estate commission but must meet local and state requirements for this subdivision.
C. A private owner may not sell only part of a single parcel; only a registered subdivider may divide land.
D. The private owner must comply with federal land sales rules.

57. The Colorado Real Estate Recovery Fund

A. provides the public with some protection if someone is financially damaged by the improper actions of a licensee.
B. supplements errors and omissions insurance in protecting licensees against losses caused by professional mistakes or illegal actions.
C. is available to repay private parties who lose money in real estate investments.
D. was replaced in 1998 by the requirement for errors and omissions insurance.

58. In Colorado, a deed of trust may be used to provide security for a real estate loan. If the deed of trust is set up with a private trustee,

A. this trustee will hold legal title to the property and be shown on the deed.
B. any foreclosure will be handled by the private trustee.
C. any foreclosure will be handled by the public trustee.
D. any foreclosure will be handled in the appropriate court.

59. Within what time period must the public trustee hold a foreclosure sale under a Colorado deed of trust arrangement?
    A. 45 to 60 days following the lender's notice of default and request for sale
    B. Whenever the court schedule permits the case to be heard
    C. Not more than 90 days following the first instance of defaulted payment
    D. Not more than six months after the lender notifies the borrower of default

60. After a public auction foreclosure sale for deed of trust default, the borrower may redeem the property any time up to
    A. 3 years.
    B. 75 days for all types of property.
    C. 75 days for all but agricultural property.
    D. 6 months for all types of property.

61. Following a foreclosure sale, the lender receives the
    A. entire proceeds of the sale, including any excess above the debt.
    B. proceeds of the sale up to the outstanding debt plus court and collection costs.
    C. uncollected loan balance only.
    D. property since it was the collateral for the loan.

62. Colorado tributary water rights and well permits are administered by the
    A. state engineer.
    B. Colorado Ground Water Commission.
    C. Colorado Supreme Court.
    D. Colorado Legislature.

63. An owner of a 35-acre parcel of undeveloped land may drill a well for water only
    A. after purchasing water rights.
    B. after obtaining a well permit from the state engineer.
    C. without any permit since a 35-acre site is entitled to an exempt well.
    D. if there is a stream on the property that may be diverted.

64. In Colorado, water rights are
    A. real property rights that automatically transfer with the land to which they are appurtenant.
    B. personal property rights that may be sold and transferred by bill of sale.
    C. personal property rights permanently affixed to the land.
    D. real property rights that may be severed and sold separately from the land.

65. Which of the following is a proper method for two or more owners of a single property in Colorado to hold title?
    A. Tenancy in severalty
    B. Joint tenancy with right of survivorship
    C. Tenancy by the entirety
    D. Community property

66. A deed purports to create a joint tenancy with right of survivorship. Which of the following would cause the deed to create tenancy in common instead?
    A. The parties receive their interests at the same time.
    B. The three parties agree to divide the property 40 percent, 30 percent, 30 percent between them.
    C. The parties agree that all have the right of possession.
    D. All parties are named on a single deed conveying the property.

67. A tenant provides proper notice and vacates an apartment. The landlord discovers substantial damage to the unit. Which of the following is a proper action by the landlord?

A. Notify the tenant that his or her damage deposit is forfeited within 60 days
B. Keep the damage deposit without notice, since the damage is obviously more than the deposit
C. Itemize the damage in writing and return any excess deposit within one month
D. Return the deposit immediately and bill the tenant for the repairs when completed

68. An out-of-state investor sells a property in Colorado. The closing entity must withhold up to 2 percent of the

A. selling price as possible income tax liability.
B. selling price as a state transfer tax.
C. net proceeds of the sale as sales tax.
D. net proceeds of the sale as possible income tax.

69. Under the Colorado Fair Housing Act, a landlord may refuse to rent a(n)

A. apartment to a single mother because the landlord is worried about who will supervise her child after school.
B. apartment to a three students because he is afraid they will have loud parties.
C. commercial space for use as a studio for African American art because the studio would "attract the wrong element."
D. unit beside the pool to a family with young children because of the danger but may offer them a unit away from the pool.

70. A real estate broker has identified a property that is ideal for a fast food outlet. He asks four friends to contribute money to the purchase and gain partial ownership. The broker will manage the property and negotiate the lease for the fast food company. In this arrangement, the broker

A. is not entitled to any commission on the purchase, since the broker will be an owner.
B. will have no liability in the deal since he will not contribute money.
C. must comply with state and federal securities laws in arranging this investment group.
D. can keep both the sales commission and the lease commission without specifically telling the others about the amounts involved.

71. Which of the following may be subject to regulation under state or federal securities laws?

A. Resort condominium project in which owners enter their units in a common rental pool to enhance their income
B. Sale of 1000 mountain sites primarily through Internet advertising
C. Condominium project that includes both residential and retail uses within one structure
D. Speculative purchase of raw land by a doctor as part of a retirement plan

72. A buyer and seller agree to write two contracts: a lower actual purchase price because the seller is under pressure to sell quickly, and a higher contract to submit for financing to allow the buyer to get a larger loan. This arrangement is
   A. good business since the parties agree and the loan can only be made if the property appraises at the higher value.
   B. fraudulent dual contracting.
   C. risky but acceptable because the lender has the right to appraise and inspect the property.
   D. acceptable for conventional loans, but not for VA or FHA loans.

73. Which is presumed to be true of a lease in Colorado?
   A. Every lease contains an implied warranty of habitability and quiet enjoyment.
   B. Every lease contains an implied warranty of quiet enjoyment only.
   C. Every lease contains an implied warranty of habitability only.
   D. Only residential leases have an implied warranty of habitability.

74. Based on the Colorado Statute of Frauds, which lease must be in writing?
   A. Month-to-month lease expected to last more than two years
   B. One-year lease for an apartment
   C. Two-year lease for commercial space
   D. Residential lease for six months that automatically converts to month-to-month after the six months

75. According to the Exclusive-Right-to-Sell Listing Contract (Residential) (Seller Agency), a broker's services include
   A. informing the seller that the seller will not be vicariously liable for the acts of the seller's broker when acting within the scope of the agency.
   B. maintaining the property in case the seller is unavailable.
   C. informing the seller that the seller will be vicariously liable for the acts of the seller's broker when acting within the scope of the agency.
   D. investigating the condition of the property on behalf of any potential buyer.

76. Based on the transaction-broker Exclusive-Right-to-Sell Listing Contract, the listing broker must disclose to any potential buyer
   A. facts about the seller actually known by broker.
   B. material facts about the property actually known by broker.
   C. all facts about the transaction actually known by broker.
   D. the motivations of seller, if requested by buyer.

77. According to the Exclusive-Right-to-Sell Listing Contract (Residential) (Seller Agency), fixtures listed on the approved form will be included
   A. unless they are crossed out on the form.
   B. if on the property at the time of the listing.
   C. if attached on the date of the listing unless specifically excluded by the seller.
   D. in every case.

78. Real estate practice in Colorado assumes that which type of deed will convey residential property, unless otherwise provided?

A. General warranty deed
B. Special warranty deed
C. Bargain and sale deed
D. Quitclaim deed

79. When completing the Exclusive-Right-to-Sell Listing Contract, which monetary encumbrances does the seller list?

A. All encumbrances to be assumed by a buyer
B. All encumbrances the seller will not pay off
C. Only encumbrances of public record
D. All encumbrances known to the seller

80. The Exclusive-Right-to-Sell listing form mentions the Seller's Property Disclosure form. The seller

A. is required by law to provide this form to every buyer.
B. may refuse to provide the disclosure and avoid disclosure of material defects.
C. may check the "As Is" box, making the buyer responsible to find any defects.
D. may decline to provide the disclosure but must still disclose latent material defects.

81. The "holdover clause" in the approved Exclusive-Right-to-Sell Listing Contract form protects the broker's commission for certain disclosed buyers

A. for up to six months after the listing expires.
B. for a negotiated time even if the seller lists the property with another broker after expiration.
C. for a negotiated time unless the seller lists the property with another broker after expiration.
D. only during the term of the listing and any extensions.

82. The Exclusive-Right-to-Sell Listing Contracts form provides several choices for the way a broker will handle an in-company transaction. Which of the following is correct?

A. The seller determines which of the three choices will apply to this listing.
B. The broker determines which of the three choices will apply to this listing.
C. Colorado law requires the seller to select an addendum.
D. Brokerage policy calls for a specific addendum, but the seller may specify that no in-company addendum will be used.

83. Based on the language of the Exclusive-Right-to-Sell Listing Contracts form, what happens if a defaulting buyer forfeits an earnest money deposit?

A. The broker and seller split the funds.
B. The broker receives the funds.
C. The seller is entitled to keep the funds.
D. The broker and seller submit the funds for mediation.

84. In the event that the seller and broker have a dispute about the Exclusive-Right-to-Sell Listing Contract, which of the following is true?

A. Both agree to submit to arbitration with the local REALTOR® association.
B. Both agree to submit the matter to binding mediation.
C. Both agree to mediation before proceeding to arbitration or litigation.
D. The matter must be resolved by a real estate commission hearing.

85. When a buyer wishes to work with a broker to locate property to purchase, the

A. buyer and broker may agree to a relationship, which could include agency, transaction-brokerage, or no working relationship between the parties.
B. buyer will be a customer with no working relationship to the brokerage company.
C. brokerage will be an agent for the buyer unless there is a written agreement for another relationship.
D. buyer and broker must sign an exclusive representation agreement.

86. Which of the following would most likely demonstrate "reasonable efforts to locate property" called for in the Exclusive-Right-to-Buy Contract?

A. Providing the buyer with addresses of Internet sites that list local properties for sale
B. Providing the buyer with descriptions of several properties recently listed with the brokerage
C. Running a "Property Wanted" ad in local newspapers
D. Showing the buyer properties that meet the general description of the property as defined in the Exclusive-Right-to-Buy Contract

87. If a broker negotiates a Success Fee under the Exclusive-Right-to-Buy Contract, which is true?

A. If the broker cannot get the fee from the listing broker or seller, the buyer is under no obligation to pay.
B. The listing broker must pay the negotiated fee at closing.
C. The broker may be directed to seek payment from any or all of several sources.
D. The buyer will pay the fee at closing.

88. Brokers working for buyers under the Exclusive-Right-to-Buy Contract may

A. also receive compensation from lenders and other service providers without disclosure to the buyer.
B. also seek a nonrefundable retainer fee, which must be credited toward any Success Fee earned.
C. negotiate an hourly fee to be paid in addition to any other compensation agreed.
D. require listing brokers to adjust their offered split to match the buyer's broker's negotiated fee.

89. According to the Exclusive-Right-to-Buy Contract, who is responsible with regard to registered sex offenders (Megan's Law)?

A. Brokers must disclose the presence of any known registered sex offenders.
B. Buyers must obtain this information from local law enforcement officials.
C. Sellers will be required to disclose any sex offenders in the neighborhood.
D. Sex offenders' privacy rights are protected by state and federal law.

90. The Inclusions and Exclusions section of the Residential Contract to Buy and Sell calls for inclusion of all of the following EXCEPT

A. window coverings on the property on the date of the sales contract.
B. leased security systems.
C. fireplace screens and grates.
D. parking and storage facilities as described in a condominium community.

91. If a buyer is assuming a loan and the loan balance turns out to be less than the assumption balance provided by the seller, the Residential Contract to Buy and Sell provides that

A. the buyer may terminate the contract by written notice if the difference causes the buyer's cash at closing to increase by a stated amount.
B. the seller must reduce the price of the property to compensate for the difference.
C. depending on how the form is completed, either the buyer may terminate the contract or the seller could reduce the price to make up for the difference.
D. the contract is automatically terminated by the seller's misrepresentation.

92. In the Purchase Price and Terms section of the Mandatory Residential Contract to Buy and Sell, the entry for cash at closing

A. represents the total amount the buyer should expect to bring to closing.
B. does not include buyer's closing costs, such as loan fees.
C. should match the good-faith estimate provided with the HUD-1 form.
D. represents the approximate amount the seller will receive at closing.

93. The approved Residential Contract to Buy and Sell establishes a loan commitment deadline if the buyer is getting a new loan. What is the effect of this deadline?

A. If the buyer cannot get a satisfactory written loan commitment, the contract terminates on that date.
B. The contract is contingent on actual funding of the new loan at closing.
C. If the buyer cannot get a satisfactory written loan commitment by that date, the buyer may terminate the contract by written notice to the seller.
D. The buyer must provide the written commitment to the seller by that date or is in default.

94. If no box is checked for the Appraisal Condition section of the Residential Contract to Buy and Sell, the

A. buyer will not have to proceed if a new loan is refused due to a low appraisal.
B. seller will have the ability to terminate the contract if the appraisal is substantially above the selling price.
C. buyer will be able to get a VA or FHA loan, but the loan will not be subject to the appraisal.
D. form has been improperly completed.

95. The Residential Contract to Buy and Sell provides an opportunity for the parties to specify that the title insurance policy provided to the buyer will have expanded coverage. If the box is checked to provide this coverage,

A. the buyer agrees to pay any additional premium for this extra protection.
B. the title insurance company may require a survey or improvement location certificate, which could increase costs to both the buyer and seller.
C. any additional premium and costs are the seller's responsibility.
D. the title company will pay to remove any defects in the title before closing.

96. The Residential Contract to Buy and Sell contains a section regarding Common Interest Community Documents. This section refers to documents for

A. multifamily housing, such as condominiums and townhomes, that have common recreational amenities.
B. any community governed by covenants.
C. communities covered by special taxing districts.
D. any community subject to mandatory assessments for maintenance of common elements.

97. Some properties may be subject to property taxes from a special taxing district serving a defined area. If buyers determine that the property is within a special taxing district, they may

A. terminate the contract by written notice to the seller.
B. demand that the seller pay the indebtedness of such a district.
C. petition to be excluded from the district.
D. terminate the contract automatically on the Off-Record Matters date.

98. The Residential Contract to Buy and Sell includes a provision about lead-based paint disclosure. According to this provision, if the building permit for a residential improvement on the property was issued prior to January 1, 1978,

A. the broker is responsible to disclose the age of the property.
B. disclosure is required only if the sellers are aware of lead-based paint on the property.
C. the contract is void unless disclosure is signed by the seller and brokers prior to the parties signing the sales contract.
D. seller and brokers must make disclosure prior to closing.

99. The Property Disclosure and Inspection provision of the Residential Contract to Buy and Sell calls for the seller to provide a Seller's Property Disclosure form based on the

A. results of a professional property inspection.
B. seller's current actual knowledge.
C. advice of the listing agent regarding the condition of the property.
D. seller's opinion of condition at the time of the contract.

100. The inspection provision of the contract to buy and sell allows the buyer to terminate the contract
   A. only if a licensed inspector determines that there are significant problems with the property.
   B. only after listing unsatisfactory conditions that cause the buyer to terminate.
   C. if the property is unsatisfactory in the buyer's subjective discretion.
   D. immediately if the seller refuses to correct certain defects.

101. Based on the inspection provision of the Residential Contract to Buy and Sell, if the buyer receives a property inspection report on the day after the Inspection Objection Deadline but the report contains several apparently serious matters, the buyer
   A. may still object because they did not have the report until after the deadline.
   B. is in default for missing the deadline, and the seller may terminate the contract.
   C. missed the opportunity to object based on inspection issues, and the contract is still in force.
   D. can compel the seller to correct these serious defects before closing.

102. A dishwasher is a fixture in the kitchen of a property that is under contract. The Seller's Property Disclosure lists the appliance as "yes" for the "In Working Condition" column. Based on the approved Residential Contract to Buy and Sell, if the dishwasher fails before closing, the seller
   A. must replace the dishwasher with a new one of similar capacity.
   B. is not responsible since he or she could not have known it would fail.
   C. must offer the buyer a credit at closing for the price of a new appliance.
   D. may replace the dishwasher with a used appliance of similar age, size, and condition.

103. During a walk-through just prior to closing, the buyers realize the carpet is much more worn than they thought. They now file an objection requiring the sellers to replace the carpet. According to the Residential Contract to Buy and Sell,
   A. the walk-through does not give them this option.
   B. since the walk-through is to verify condition, this objection is proper.
   C. they may do this even if the Inspection Objection Deadline has passed.
   D. the sellers will have a reasonable period of time following closing to comply.

104. The Contract to Buy and Sell states that "time is of the essence hereof." This statement means that

A. everything in the contract must be complete within one year, or it will be void.
B. all dates and deadlines must be performed within a reasonable margin of the stated time or date.
C. everything not done by closing will be waived.
D. dates and deadlines will be strictly interpreted.

105. If a Residential Contract to Buy and Sell form is marked to indicate the "Liquidated Damages" choice in case the buyer is in default, the

A. earnest money and any other payments or things of value received from the buyer will be kept by the seller as seller's sole remedy for buyer's default.
B. seller may keep earnest money and also sue for actual damages resulting from the buyer's default.
C. buyer may cure the default by offering money.
D. seller may be able to sue the buyer to force the buyer to perform under the contract.

106. If a dispute over the Residential Contract to Buy and Sell goes to court, the contract says that court costs and legal fees shall be

A. awarded to the broker.
B. awarded to the losing party.
C. split evenly between the parties.
D. awarded to the winning party.

107. In the event of a dispute between the parties relating to the Contract to Buy and Sell, the parties

A. must mediate in good faith to seek a settlement for up to 30 days.
B. may immediately decide to mediate or seek arbitration or litigation.
C. must accept the solution presented by the qualified mediator chosen by the parties.
D. must submit the dispute to arbitration if mediation is unsuccessful.

108. When are facsimile signatures on the Contract to Buy and Sell acceptable?

A. By rule of the real estate commission
B. If the parties agree and indicate that choice on the contract form
C. Only during negotiation and not at closing
D. In no case

109. Various provisions of the Residential Contract to Buy and Sell call for notification to one of the parties about various events or objections. According to the wording of the approved form, notice

A. must be directly to the party and not its broker.
B. to the party must be by "normal channels of communication," such as telephone, mail, or facsimile.
C. is effective when received by either the party or the broker working with that party.
D. may be sent to the broker but is effective only when received by the party.

110. When a seller receives an offer from a buyer, the seller may properly respond by
   A. writing "rejected" at the top and signing it at the bottom on the appropriate seller line.
   B. checking an appropriate box, initialing the form, and submitting a counterproposal.
   C. telling his or her broker to call the buyer with a counteroffer.
   D. telling his or her broker to call the buyer with his or her acceptance.

111. When a broker signs the Broker Acknowledgements at the end of the Residential Contract to Buy and Sell, the broker
   A. becomes a party to the contract and agrees to its terms.
   B. assures the right to a commission.
   C. acknowledges receipt of the earnest money deposit.
   D. confirms the commission split with cooperating brokers.

112. According to the Colorado Real Estate Commission Position Statement regarding Rule F,
   A. brokers may not add exculpatory language to any commission-approved contract.
   B. exculpatory language limiting the broker's liability may be added to the Contract to Buy and Sell only in addenda, not in additional provisions.
   C. brokers may not add exculpatory language limiting their liability to the Contract to Buy and Sell.
   D. exculpatory language limiting a broker's liability may not appear in listings or buyer relationship agreements.

113. The Colorado Real Estate Commission has approved a broad variety of standard forms and made their use mandatory by licensees. Which of the following is one of the primary reasons for these forms?
   A. Assists attorneys and members of the public in following commission rules when contracting
   B. Assures the broker's compliance with the Conway-Bogue decision of the Colorado Supreme Court
   C. Allows the commission to discipline brokers for improper contracting
   D. Protects the public by requiring the same forms for all real estate transactions in Colorado

114. When a broker has a seller agency listing, which would permit the broker or any associates in the broker's office to show that listing to a potential buyer who is not working with another broker?
   A. The seller has signed a Transaction-Broker Addendum to the listing.
   B. There are no special requirements since this is what the listing is all about.
   C. The seller has signed a Transaction-Broker Addendum, and the buyer is willing to sign a Dual Agency Addendum.
   D. The buyer must sign an exclusive Transaction-Broker agreement.

115. What disclosure is required when a buyer's agent approaches a for-sale-by-owner on behalf of the buyer client?
   A. No disclosure since the seller has elected to be unrepresented
   B. None as long as the broker seeks to list the property prior to submitting the buyer's offer
   C. Disclosure of the broker's working relationship with the buyer
   D. Disclosure of the buyer's financial capability to complete a purchase

116. Which of the following requires the use of the Licensee Buyout Addendum to the Contract to Buy and Sell?
   A. A broker wishes to acquire a property he or she has listed to use as an investment.
   B. An associate in the listing brokerage company wishes to purchase a property listed by another associate.
   C. An associate is offering a guarantee buyout arrangement as an inducement to list with his or her company.
   D. A listing associate offers to purchase a property immediately after the listing expires.

117. When is the listing brokerage company responsible for a guaranteed buyout agreement under the Licensee Buyout Addendum to the Contract to Buy and Sell?
   A. If the principal broker signs at the bottom of the addendum
   B. When the buyout date arrives
   C. Only if the listing associate is unable to perform the buyout
   D. When the buyout is for the personal use of the principal broker

118. Which of the following is appropriate when the licensee wishes to extend the effective period for a listing agreement?
   A. Agreement to Amend/Extend Contract
   B. Agreement to Amend/Extend Contract with Broker
   C. Extension letter prepared on company stationery and signed by the seller
   D. Alter the date on the original listing and have both seller and broker initial the change

119. What is the primary difference between the commission-approved deed of trust forms?
   A. Forms are specific for residential, agricultural, and investment loans.
   B. Forms are specific for public trustee or private trustee transactions.
   C. Forms contain different provisions for assumption of the loan upon sale of the property.
   D. Forms contain different provisions depending on the loan program to be used for funding the loan.

120. The approved Earnest Money Promissory Note
   A. should not be used because earnest money should be in good funds.
   B. must be due early enough to assure good funds for closing.
   C. should be accompanied by any of the three deed of trust forms.
   D. allows the seller to sue for the earnest money in case the closing fails.

121. If a seller has signed a Transaction-Broker Addendum to an Exclusive-Right-to-Sell Listing Contract, when the addendum provisions are triggered, what major agency duty is removed?
   A. The duty to communicate material facts
   B. The duty of the broker to advise the Seller on the choices available
   C. The duty of the broker to investigate information provided by the buyer
   D. The duty to maintain the seller's motivations as confidential information

122. When an Earnest Money Promissory Note is used to provide earnest money, another condition that must be met includes that the
   A. buyer must provide a financial statement to qualify for the note.
   B. note must be specifically mentioned in the contract along with the due date.
   C. note must be held by the buyer's broker until it is honored.
   D. listing broker will be responsible to sue the buyer if the note is not honored.

123. According to the commission-approved Exclusive-Right-to-Sell Listing Contract, how is a broker's compensation determined?
   A. Set by the real estate commission for certain geographic areas
   B. Set by the local brokers as a standard fee
   C. Established by the seller
   D. Established by the broker

124. An in-company transaction is one in which a broker
   A. has an agency listing, and the cooperating broker is a transaction-broker.
   B. is agent for the seller, and the buyer is a customer.
   C. represents or is working with both parties to a transaction.
   D. is agent for the buyer with no working relationship with the seller.

125. Regarding company policy concerning agency for in-company or in-house transactions, a broker may not represent sellers
   A. as seller's agent and buyers as transaction-broker.
   B. as seller's agent and buyers as customers.
   C. as seller's agent and buyers as buyer's agent (dual agency).
   D. and buyers as transaction-broker for either or both.

126. A licensee lists a property using an approved Exclusive-Right-to-Sell Listing Contract, shows the property to a potential buyer, and provides that buyer's name to the seller in writing. After the listing expires, the sellers list exclusively with another broker. The buyers return to the original listing agent to prepare an offer on the property. If they buy, who is legally entitled to the commission?
   A. Original listing agent, because it is within the holdover period
   B. Original listing agent, because he or she is the procuring cause of the sale
   C. The new listing broker earns the listing side only.
   D. The new listing broker earns it all and may agree to split it with the original listing broker.

127. How would an associate broker with Realty, Inc., complete the name of the broker in the blank on the Exclusive-Right-to-Sell Listing Contract?
   A. Associate Broker, agent for Realty, Inc.
   B. Associate Broker, Colorado License AB67123
   C. Realty, Inc.
   D. Realty, Inc. per Associate

128. While holding an Exclusive-Right-to-Sell Listing Contract, the licensee
   - A. agrees to work exclusively with this seller and no others at the same time.
   - B. cannot work with buyers who might be interested in the seller's property.
   - C. must sell this seller's property to comply with the agreement.
   - D. has permission to work with other sellers at the same time.

129. Company policy calls for dual agency for in-company transactions. After the Dual Agency Addendum is signed, the
   - A. licensee's fiduciary duties are modified for any sale of the property.
   - B. seller may not depend on the licensee to keep the seller's motivations confidential.
   - C. seller has no vicarious liability for the licensee's actions.
   - D. licensee has the seller's consent to represent another principal in the same transaction.

130. When a broker and buyer enter into an Exclusive-Right-to-Buy Contract, the
   - A. buyer may have such agreements with several brokers.
   - B. broker is bound to work with only one buyer at a time.
   - C. broker must be a buyer's agent.
   - D. buyer is bound to work with one broker during the term of the contract.

131. In an Exclusive-Right-to-Buy Contract (Buyer Agency) agreement, regarding the commission, the
   - A. buyer must pay the broker's commission since payment determines agency.
   - B. broker can force the seller to pay by writing it in the offer.
   - C. buyer's broker can often share in the listing broker's fee to obtain compensation.
   - D. buyer agent's commission should equal a full listing commission paid by a seller.

132. After signing an Exclusive-Right-to-Sell Contract (Seller Agency), the listing broker must also disclose
   - A. broker obligations to the seller.
   - B. the amount and source of listing commission to any buyer.
   - C. to any prospective buyer the listing broker's agency to the seller.
   - D. all material defects, known or unknown.

133. The approved Exclusive-Agency Listing Contract
   - A. eliminates the broker's confidentiality duties.
   - B. allows the seller to negotiate a sale and not pay the broker.
   - C. allows the seller to sell after the listing period to anyone without paying commission.
   - D. removes the seller's vicarious liability for activities of the broker.

134. All of the following must be in compliance with a broker's escrow or trust account EXCEPT
   A. by being maintained in the name of the licensed brokerage.
   B. by being insured by agency of the federal government.
   C. by having only the broker authorized to withdraw funds.
   D. by being reconciled regularly to guard against commingling.

135. In a transaction with a listing broker and a buyer's agent broker, who holds the earnest money deposit?
   A. Listing broker
   B. Buyer's broker
   C. Must be in a neutral escrow company
   D. The brokers establish a joint escrow.

136. What shows all deposits and payments to and from a broker's escrow account in chronological order?
   A. Bank reconciliation
   B. Ledger cards
   C. Bank statement
   D. Account journal

137. One-half of the general property tax has been paid by February 28; by what date must the balance be paid to avoid penalty?
   A. March 1
   B. March 31
   C. April 30
   D. June 15

138. A broker keeps one or more escrow or trust accounts in order to
   A. keep money from each sales transaction separate from all other transactions.
   B. make internal bookkeeping easier.
   C. assure that he or she is receiving the proper interest on these funds.
   D. segregate funds belonging to others from brokerage operating funds.

139. The Closing Instructions form (CL8-9-95)
   A. may be used only by title insurance companies.
   B. must be part of every contract.
   C. provides for the closing company to give legal advice to the listing broker.
   D. engages a closing service on behalf of the buyer and seller.

140. According to statute, "good funds" include a
   A. check drawn on the broker's escrow account.
   B. teller's check from a savings and loan.
   C. title insurance company corporate check.
   D. check from the buyer that will clear the bank.

141. If a buyer and seller have a dispute over earnest money, the listing broker may
   A. hold the money in the escrow account until the parties provide mutual instructions.
   B. immediately issue a check to the seller who has employed the broker.
   C. interplead the money so the court may award all transaction expenses to the broker.
   D. divide the money between buyer and seller on an equitable basis.

142. If the buyer notifies the seller in writing of a termination of the contract under the Loan Commitment Deadline provision, what happens to the earnest money?
   A. The broker must hold it until she gets mutual agreement to return it to the buyer.
   B. Since the buyer could not get a loan, the money goes to the seller.
   C. The broker must immediately return the money to the buyer.
   D. The buyer and seller will mediate any disagreement about earnest money.

143. Following closing, a listing broker should pay commissions due to company associates
   A. immediately from the escrow account to close the ledger at zero.
   B. from the company operating account according to employment agreements.
   C. from the escrow account at the end of the accounting period.
   D. after withholding independent contractor taxes and contributions.

144. What is the listing broker's responsibility for an earnest money promissory note?
   A. Hold the note until closing, at which time it will be redeemed
   B. Sue for payment if the buyer does not redeem the note when due
   C. Hold the note, and notify the seller if the note is not redeemed on time
   D. Deliver the note to the seller until it is redeemed

145. When must an independent broker first open a trust account?
   A. When applying for a license in that status
   B. When joining the local board of REALTOR®
   C. When the broker first receives earnest money to deposit
   D. Before activating an inactive license

146. If a broker has an interest-bearing trust account, the interest
   A. earned belongs to the broker.
   B. may accrue to a nonprofit affordable housing fund.
   C. earned will belong to the seller.
   D. earned may be applied to closing costs.

147. In connection with property management activities, security deposits
   A. must be held by the property owner, not the manager.
   B. may be held in the management trust account.
   C. should be held in a separate, security deposit trust account by the property manager.
   D. are normally used for property expenses until needed for return to the tenant.

148. May a property manager have a single escrow account for several properties and several owners?
   A. No, because this is illegal commingling of multiple clients' money
   B. Yes, but the manager must not let any owner's balance go below zero.
   C. Only if all owners receive a copy of the monthly bank statement
   D. Yes, if all owners give specific permission for this arrangement

149. The Colorado Real Estate Commission may audit a broker's files

A. only after 72 hours notice by certified mail.
B. only when a specific complaint has been filed.
C. at any time, without notice.
D. when confirming license renewal.

150. A broker must keep transaction file records

A. until the brokerage goes out of business.
B. and so must the associate involved with the transaction.
C. in the office for up to 17 years, then in the state archive.
D. readily accessible for four years.

151. The Statement of Settlement prepared for the closing must be signed by

A. only the seller or buyer.
B. the licensee who personally established a brokerage relationship with the party.
C. both employing brokers.
D. the buyer, seller, closing company, and listing broker on each form.

152. When must a listing broker deposit an earnest money check?

A. Within one business day of receipt from a prospective buyer
B. Not later than the acceptance date on the offer
C. Not later than one business day after learning of acceptance of the offer
D. Within seven days after acceptance of the offer

153. If an earnest money check is not honored by the buyer's bank, the broker should

A. deposit it again to see if it will clear the second time.
B. file notice under Colorado's bad check law for treble damages.
C. notify the buyer's broker that the contract is canceled due to the buyer's default.
D. notify the seller and ask what they wish to do next.

154. The listing contract is preserved in whose transaction files?

A. Selling broker only
B. Listing broker only
C. Both listing and selling brokers
D. Title company, listing broker, and selling broker

155. A broker's trust account at a well-financed credit union

A. is entirely proper if it is set up according to commission rules.
B. does not offer the proper insurance protection to the account beneficiaries.
C. pays a higher rate of interest to the broker than commercial bank accounts.
D. has the required federal deposit insurance from the FDIC.

156. The six-column settlement worksheet entry for the property purchase price would be

A. debit the seller, credit the broker.
B. debit the seller, credit the buyer.
C. credit the seller, debit the buyer.
D. credit the seller, debit the broker.

157. How is a buyer's earnest money deposit treated at closing?

A. The buyer gets credit for the deposit as part of the purchase price.
B. The seller is debited the earnest money amount as already paid.
C. The broker gets credited with the deposit that is brought to closing.
D. The deposit has no effect on closing as it was already deposited.

158. A loan being assumed by a buyer has what effect at closing?

A. Debit the seller, credit the broker
B. Debit the seller, credit the buyer
C. Credit the seller, debit the buyer
D. Credit the seller, debit the broker

159. If the seller agrees to carry back part of the purchase price as a second deed of trust, what is the effect at closing?

A. Credit the seller who will receive this money later from the buyer
B. Credit the buyer who can use this promise to pay in place of cash at closing
C. Credit the broker who must account for this noncash payment
D. No entry on the settlement sheet, since this is not a cash amount at closing

160. If the buyer is assuming an 8.5 percent loan with a balance of $127,538.00 at a closing on July 11, what is the interest proration?

A. $291.42 debit the seller, credit the buyer
B. $297.01 debit the seller, credit the buyer
C. $611.98 debit the seller, credit the buyer
D. $623.71 debit the seller, credit the buyer

161. Based on the approved Contract to Buy and Sell, the title insurance premium would be entered on a settlement worksheet as

A. debit the seller, credit the broker.
B. debit the seller, credit the buyer.
C. credit the seller, debit the buyer.
D. credit the seller, debit the broker.

162. On the settlement worksheet, charges for "Abstracting: Before sale" would include

A. an abstract certified to date by a qualified abstractor.
B. an abstractor entering the warranty deed on the abstract.
C. a buyer's attorney providing an opinion of title.
D. the recording fee for any release of an existing deed of trust.

163. How would the charges for an attorney to examine the title documents normally appear on the settlement worksheet?

A. Debit the seller, credit the broker
B. Debit the seller, credit the buyer
C. Credit the broker, debit the buyer
D. Credit the seller, debit the broker

164. At closing, who normally is charged for the recording charges for the warranty deed?

A. Seller
B. Buyer
C. Broker
D. Lender

165. The six-column settlement worksheet would show the charges for recording a deed of trust as

A. debit the buyer, credit the broker.
B. debit the seller, credit the buyer.
C. credit the seller, debit the buyer.
D. credit the seller, debit the broker.

166. A broker is informed of an $18 charge for recording a release of deed of trust in connection with a loan to be paid off at closing. This charge would be entered as

A. debit the seller, credit the buyer.
B. debit the buyer, credit the seller.
C. debit the seller, credit the broker.
D. debit the buyer, credit the broker.

167. If a Colorado property sells for $245,900, what documentary fee will be paid when the warranty deed is recorded?

A. $24.59
B. $25.00
C. $245.90
D. $250.00

168. A broker is requested to order a Certificate of Taxes Due at a cost of $22. How does this appear on the settlement worksheet?

A. $22 debit the seller, credit the broker
B. $22 debit the buyer, credit the broker
C. $11 debit the seller, $11 debit the buyer, $22 credit the broker
D. No entry, this is paid outside of closing.

169. If the taxes for the preceding year are unpaid at the time of an August 14 closing, what must the broker do?

A. Debit the full amount plus penalties to the seller and pay the county
B. Prorate to August 14 for the benefit of the buyer
C. Debit the full amount plus penalties to the seller and credit the buyer
D. Nothing, these taxes will be due during the following January

170. If taxes for the preceding year are unpaid as of a closing on February 23 and the closing involves a cash sale, what must the broker do?

A. Debit the seller and credit the buyer for the full amount
B. Debit the seller, credit the broker for the full amount, and pay the taxes
C. No closing entry is needed, but the broker must demand that seller pay the taxes before the end of April
D. Prorate the taxes to February 23

171. If taxes for the preceding year have not been paid as of a closing on February 23 and the closing involves a new loan, what must the broker do?

A. Debit the seller the full amount, credit the broker, and pay the taxes
B. Debit the seller and credit the buyer the full amount
C. Check with the new lender for its method of handling these taxes
D. Prorate the taxes to February 23

172. If the real estate taxes for last year were $3,685 what would the prorated tax entry be for this year's taxes for a September 11 closing?

A. $1,130.74 debit to the seller, $2,554.26 credit to the buyer
B. $1,130.75 debit to the buyer, $2,554.26 credit to the seller
C. $2,554.26 debit to the seller, $2,554.26 credit to the buyer
D. $2,554.26 debit to the seller, $2,554.26 credit to the broker

173. Under what circumstances would the settlement statement reflect no proration for this year's taxes?
   A. The seller already paid them in April for a closing May 1 or later.
   B. For a December 31 closing
   C. For a January 1 closing
   D. A buyer is getting a new loan.

174. What does a Tax Reserve entry on line 19 of the settlement worksheet indicate?
   A. The broker has withheld this amount of tax money to give back to the seller.
   B. There is an existing loan being assumed with a reserve balance to transfer to the buyer.
   C. An amount of prorated taxes to transfer to the buyer
   D. A seller's obligation to the existing lender, which must be satisfied at closing

175. In a new loan closing, the settlement worksheet will show an entry for a tax reserve that indicates the new lender is
   A. collecting this tax amount from the seller.
   B. deducting this amount as a loan transfer fee.
   C. withholding this amount from loan proceeds to start the impound account for the next payment of taxes.
   D. contributing this amount toward the buyer's taxes for this year.

176. A special tax or special assessment is shown on the Certificate of Taxes due in the amount of $834 for a curb and gutter project. The tax is payable over 10 years with annual interest of five percent. If the buyer has agreed to assume this property obligation, how will it show on the settlement worksheet?
   A. It will not show up, since it has no financial effect on the closing.
   B. $834 debit to the seller, $834 credit to the buyer
   C. $834 debit to the seller, $834 credit to the broker
   D. $834 plus prorated interest debit to the seller and credit to the buyer

177. A tax certificate shows a special assessment tax of $1,123 on a property for which the buyer is getting a new loan. What will most likely show up on the settlement worksheet at closing?
   A. $1,123 debit to the seller and credit to the buyer
   B. $1,123 debit to the seller and credit to the broker
   C. $1,123 debit to the seller, single entry on the settlement worksheet
   D. No entry. Special assessments do not show up on the settlement worksheet.

178. In Colorado, personal property taxes apply to
   A. personal property used in business, such as office furniture or copy machines.
   B. personal property attached to real property as fixtures and transferred in a sale.
   C. the sale of new personal property.
   D. personal property, such as a refrigerator, included in a residential sale.

179. Assumption of an existing hazard insurance policy is

A. common in residential sales.
B. common in commercial sales, but not residential sales.
C. uncommon due to problems with coverage and insurance contracts.
D. prohibited by the insurance commission.

180. If an FHA loan is being assumed, the FHA Mortgage Insurance Premium (MIP)

A. is always collected monthly, and the monthly premium is prorated.
B. may have been paid up front and financed into the loan, which requires no proration.
C. will be collected again from the new borrower and so is not subject to proration or refund.
D. depends on the age and type of FHA loan and must be carefully calculated.

181. If the settlement worksheet contains a figure for "Mortgage Insurance Reserve," it probably means that

A. an old balance remains, which will be refunded to the seller.
B. annual mortgage insurance premiums are being collected in an impound account for future payment.
C. the mortgage insurance has been canceled, and an excess amount was collected. This excess belongs to the mortgage insurer.
D. the buyer will receive a credit for amounts the seller has already paid.

182. Loan discount points

A. are always paid by the buyer as costs of borrowing.
B. are always paid by the seller because of lender's rules.
C. may be paid by the buyer, the seller, or a combination of the two.
D. are tax deductible only to the seller.

183. A lender who offers a loan at 7.5 percent with three loan discount points is probably anticipating a yield on the loan of approximately

A. 7.53%.
B. 7.675%.
C. 7.875%.
D. 8.0%.

184. A lender is charging three discount points on an 80% loan for a $275,000 sale. The broker is instructed to charge two points to the seller. The settlement sheet entry would appear as

A. $4,400 debit seller, credit broker.
B. $4,400 debit seller, single entry.
C. $5,500 debit seller, credit broker.
D. $5,500 debit seller, single entry.

185. A buyer assumes the seller's existing loan and gets a new seller-carry second loan for $45,000 at 9 percent interest with monthly payments. If the first payment is due October 1 and the closing is August 17, what is the settlement sheet entry for Line 29 "Interest on New Loan"?

A. No entry; this line is for new first loans.
B. $166.44 debit buyer, credit broker
C. $166.44 debit buyer, credit seller
D. $163.31 debit buyer, credit seller

186. Who pays for a survey ordered after the date of the purchase contract?

A. Buyer
B. Seller
C. It is negotiable—check the contract
D. Lender

187. If a water bill is based on a water meter reading, how is the bill handled at closing?

A. The water bill is prorated based on an average of recent bills.
B. Water is a utility that doesn't need to be dealt with at closing.
C. The broker should withhold an amount sufficient to pay the seller's final bill.
D. The last actual bill is prorated based on the seller's time in the property since then.

188. A water bill is due in advance for the period September 1 through November 30. The amount of the bill is $129. As of the date of closing, September 9, the bill is unpaid. How should the broker handle this on the settlement worksheet?

A. $129 debit to seller, credit to buyer
B. $117.66 debit to seller, credit to buyer
C. $11.34 debit to seller, $117.66 debit to buyer, $129 credit to broker
D. $11.34 debit to seller, $129 credit to buyer

189. A water bill is due in arrears for the period March 14 to May 15 in the amount of $47. For a closing on May 8, how will the settlement worksheet reflect this bill?

A. $4.62 debit to buyer, credit to seller
B. $41.69 debit to seller, credit to buyer
C. $42.38 debit to seller, credit to buyer
D. $42.38 debit to buyer, credit to seller

190. An investor is buying a duplex with rents due on the first of the month. At the time of a closing on June 7, the $475 rent on unit A has been paid, and the $525 rent on unit B has not been paid. The investor agrees to pursue the collection of unit B's rent. How will the rents be treated on the settlement worksheet?

A. $485 debit to seller, credit to buyer
B. $380 debit to seller, $105 debit to buyer
C. $275 debit to seller, credit to buyer
D. $420 debit seller, $380 credit buyer

191. An investor buyer is acquiring a fourplex property. Each unit has a $300 security deposit held by the seller. How are these deposits handled on the settlement worksheet?

A. $1,200 debit seller, credit broker
B. $1,200 debit seller, credit buyer
C. $1,200 debit buyer, credit seller
D. No entry. The deposits are returned to the tenants, and the new owner collects new deposits.

192. A closing is scheduled for October 4 with an existing loan to be assumed. The lender informs the broker that the October 1 payment has not been made as of October 3. The seller says the payment was mailed on October 2. How should the broker proceed with the settlement worksheet?

A. Debit the seller and credit the broker the full payment that will be refunded by the lender
B. Debit the seller and credit the buyer the full payment, which will pay down the loan by an extra payment
C. Make no entry, since the lender will get the payment in the mail soon
D. Postpone the closing until the lender revises the assumption figures

193. How is the broker's fee normally shown on the settlement statement?

A. Debit the seller, credit the buyer
B. Debit the seller, credit the broker
C. Debit the seller, single entry since broker will keep it
D. Debit seller and buyer equally, credit the broker the full amount

194. In a new loan closing, the net loan proceeds after the lender subtracts loan fees and closing costs are entered on the settlement worksheet

A. credit the buyer, debit the broker.
B. credit the buyer, debit the seller.
C. debit the broker, single entry.
D. credit the broker, single entry.

195. In a new loan closing, where is the gross amount of the new loan entered on the settlement worksheet?

A. It is not entered, since the net loan proceeds will show up from the lender at closing.
B. Credit the buyer and debit the broker on the "Trust deed payable to:" line.
C. Credit the buyer, single entry on the "Trust deed payable to:" line.
D. Credit the buyer, debit the seller on the "Trust deed payable to:" line.

196. At closing, who is responsible to confirm the figures on the Statement of Settlement presented to the buyer?

A. Listing broker
B. Listing licensee who created the brokerage relationship on behalf of the listing broker
C. Selling licensee who created the brokerage relationship on behalf of the selling broker
D. Both the listing broker and the selling licensee

197. A buyer's broker attends closing and discovers that his or her buyer was charged $225 for an appraisal the seller had agreed to pay for. How should the broker handle this?

A. Ignore it since all the paperwork has these numbers on it
B. Stop the closing and demand all new settlement statements and good funds figures
C. Suggest that if the buyer agrees, the seller could give the buyer a personal check for this amount to settle this unfortunate oversight
D. Demand that the listing broker pay this amount since they should have caught the error

198. A listing broker arrives at closing and discovers that an easement release that the title company requires from a neighbor's lender is missing. The title representative indicates that she confirmed that it had been sent, but it has not yet arrived. What should the listing broker do?

A. Reschedule the closing for a few days later and wait for this release
B. Insist that the title insurance company go ahead without the release, which may leave a minor exclusion in the title insurance policy
C. Insist that the title company get another release sent by courier while everyone waits
D. Suggest that if everything else is in order, the settlement could proceed "in escrow" with the title company instructed to actually close when the release is received

199. If you are unable to attend a closing for a transaction in which you established the brokerage relationship on behalf of your broker, you should

A. apologize, but explain that you don't really need to be there anyway.
B. ask another licensee in your office to attend for you and share the responsibility to confirm the buyer's closing figures.
C. inform the listing agent that he or she will be totally responsible for the closing.
D. postpone the closing to a time more convenient for you.

200. A property sold for $200,000 but was heavily encumbered. This left the seller with only $4,500 cash proceeds at the closing. The seller is an out of state investor and is subject to the Colorado Department of Revenue income tax withholding. How much should the closing company withhold?

A. $90
B. $4,000
C. $4,500
D. $6,000

Answer Key

1. C. Private owners may always act for themselves and are not subject to real estate license laws. Attorneys are normally exempt from real estate license law while practicing law but must have a license to act as a broker. An inactive licensee is still bound by all rules of the commission, and the right-of-way specialist is exempt only for certain specific activities.

2. D. The commission's function is to protect the public through licensing of brokers and enforcing the licensing law through rules, forms, and disciplinary proceedings. Broker's commissions are negotiated and subject to contract law and civil litigation. The commission does not provide mediation or legal advice in settling disputes.

3. B. If the commission staff determines that a violation may have occurred, the commission may refer the matter to a formal hearing before an administrative law judge. If the judge finds that the license law was violated, the commission will set an appropriate penalty. Penalties may include public censure, license suspension, license revocation, and/or a fine of not more than $2,500. The commission has no authority to determine damages or order restitution.

4. A. The law requires investigation of verified written complaints. A licensee convicted of a crime could be investigated if the crime is related to real estate activities or qualification. There are no "quotas" for levels of investigation, and the commission does not deal with commission disputes between brokers.

5. C. In order to be the broker of record for a corporation, the only requirement is to have a valid, active Colorado broker's license. A March 2001 law removed the requirements for ownership and officer/director status.

6. B. Regarding a corporate brokerage, the temporary hardship license can only be issued to someone currently licensed in Colorado (broker or salesperson). The requirements for ownership and director status are waived. Since a sole proprietorship has no business entity to continue, someone would need to establish a new brokerage entity and rehire all employed licensees and renegotiate all listings.

7. D. If the employing broker fails to notify the commission of the address change in writing, all licenses in the company will be inactive until the change is made. One notification serves for the broker and all associated licensees.

8. B. Colorado license renewal is on a three-year cycle with expiration on December 31 of that year. No examination is required.

9. A. Every active Colorado licensee must have errors and omissions insurance coverage. Inactive licensees are not required to carry E&O insurance; however, they must remember that they cannot conduct any real estate activities, either. Employing broker business entities must also have coverage independent of the personal coverage for the broker of record.

10. C. The requirement is for 24 hours of approved continuing education, including an eight-hour mandatory course required by the commission. The real estate commission must approve the course and the provider.

11. C. Renewal of an inactive license requires payment of the normal renewal fee. While inactive, the licensee does not need continuing education or errors and omissions insurance. Inactive licensees may not perform any brokerage function but are fully subject to the control and discipline of the real estate commission.

12. C. An independent broker under Colorado law may work independently without the supervision of another broker.

13. B. The commission requires that the brokerage entity, as licensed with the commission, be advertised at least as prominently as the franchise or trade group identity. This practice helps the public identify the responsible brokerage.

14. D. The licensee must include the name of her employing broker. All advertising must include the employing broker's name.

15. D. The commission rules regarding advertising of brokerage identity all apply to any Web site or Internet advertising. As long as the public can clearly identify the brokerage entity, the requirements are satisfied.

16. A. All advertising by an employed licensee must include the identity of the brokerage that holds the associate's license. This requirement is not specific to the Internet.

17. B. Net listings are legal in Colorado, but they can lead to problems because of conflicts of interest between the seller and broker. Brokers are still responsible for an accurate representation of value and for the statutory duties of either an agent or transaction-broker.

18. D. Commissions are always negotiable between the principal and the agent. The commissions are not determined by law, the real estate commission, or by a group of local brokers.

19. A. Commissions are always negotiable between the principal and the agent and are not determined by custom or law. The commission may be not be shared with an unlicensed party nor be deducted from the earnest money deposit.

20. C. Earnest money must be deposited on the first business day after the broker learns of acceptance of the offer. Property management funds, such as rent and security deposits, are subject to different time limits.

21. D. Between the time that the offer is received and accepted, the earnest money should be held in a secure place in the broker's real estate office. Once the offer is accepted, the broker may deposit this buyer's funds into an escrow account containing money from other customers and clients. The account may be interest bearing: either with specific agreement of the beneficiaries or for the interest to go an approved housing opportunity fund.

22. D. The broker may not commingle this deposit with personal funds; the broker must use a proper escrow or trust account. Any interest earned must be paid according to an agreement with the parties to the transaction or to an authorized housing opportunity fund.

23. A. The escrow account checks must be identified as such and must have the name of the brokerage entity. The responsible broker's name must be on the account but does not need to be on the checks for a corporate or partnership account. The escrow account may be in the same bank as the broker's personal checking account; both must be clearly identified.

24. C. The broker improperly commingled funds and is in violation of regulations. When the broker used funds from the other account, the broker actually used another client's funds for the repair. A broker would not normally be expected to use personal funds for such a repair.

25. B. The listing agreement may be canceled, but the seller may be responsible for some expenses. The real estate commission will not be involved.

26. B. Salespeople and employed brokers may collect compensation only from their employing brokers.

27. D. The employed licensee and employing broker have a joint responsibility to assure that the commission is notified of any change of employment status. Only one notice is required.

28. A. A salesperson or associate broker may be licensed with only one broker.

29. D. It is a violation of commission regulations to accept the money. The associate broker acted improperly. A salesperson may collect a fee only from his or her employing broker. If the employing broker decided to give the money to the associate, it still had to pass through the employing broker's account.

30. D. If the broker's license is suspended or revoked, all the salespersons' and associate brokers' licenses are on inactive status until the salespersons and associate brokers are "hired" by a new broker.

31. C. Independent brokers and employing brokers must keep records from their brokerage activities for four years.

32. A. The employing broker has specific supervisory requirements for all employed licensees. Rules E-30, E-31, and E-32 apply to supervision of all employed licensees. Rule E-29 makes it clear that "employed licensee" applies to commission rules and license law. It does not infer any particular status for other things such as income taxation.

33. C. The Colorado Real Estate Commission has stated that there is no public harm in a referral fee to an unlicensed party as long as that party does nothing that requires a license. They caution that RESPA regulations may have more strict rules regarding referral fees.

34. D. If the broker has a brokerage working relationship in the transaction, the fee must be disclosed, and the broker's principal must agree. The real estate commission cautions that RESPA regulations may have more strict rules regarding referral fees from a mortgage person.

35. B. Real estate commission rules specifically forbid such fees. In addition, Insurance Division rules prohibit title companies from offering such incentives.

36. D. The law requires disclosure in writing at the earliest practical moment. The commission allows conversation to build rapport, but you must disclose an agency relationship before receiving or eliciting any confidential information from the prospective buyer.

37. A. A buyer's agent must inform the for sale by owner in writing at the first physical meeting or orally, if first contact was on the phone, that the agent represents the buyer, not the seller. The commission has approved a specific disclosure form for this situation.

38. C. As a transaction-broker working with the seller, the licensee will automatically owe the same statutory duties to any unrepresented buyer. The licensee must disclose this in writing unless the licensee also enters into an exclusive working relationship with the buyer before providing services.

39. D. In another transaction, the sellers may hire the licensee as either an agent or a transaction-broker. This is not related to the previous relationship. The licensee must be aware that the sellers may expect "agency" service even if the licensee decides on transaction-broker status.

40. B. Commission rules place primary responsibility for a transaction with the listing broker. Earnest money checks should be made payable to the listing broker and turned over to the listing broker along with the offer. Selling brokers should keep a copy of the check and get a receipt from the listing broker.

41. D. The associate broker must disclose that he or she has a real estate license. Since the associate broker's broker has potential responsibility in all of his or her real estate transactions, the broker needs to know what is going on. The property need not be listed.

42. C. A physical address must be in commission records, and office files must be there for inspection. While the rules call for a location "open to the public," they do not specify any particular hours.

43. D. The Colorado Supreme Court decided that the practice of filling in blanks by real estate licensees is authorized, but that it still constitutes the practice of law.

44. A. The license law specifically prohibits representing one party as agent and the other party as transaction-broker in the same transaction. The duties of an agent conflict with the duties of a transaction-broker.

45. C. Completing a market analysis does not require a license. The licensed associate must present it and disclose the identity of the preparer. Activities that require a license include showing properties to buyers, completing forms with consumers, and independently hosting an open house.

46. B. An unlicensed personal assistant may distribute literature prepared by a licensee. It is acceptable for an unlicensed personal assistant to chauffeur the buyers if a licensee will show the property. The assistant may complete, but not present, the market analysis.

47. A. All available offers must be presented and reviewed. The order of receipt is immaterial. The seller has the right to see each to compare offers.

48. A. Since the buyer is working with another company, no in-company conflict is involved, and the agency stays in place. The addendum is not necessary for this buyer.

49. C. Advising a particular course of action is the unauthorized practice of law. Leaving it blank is temporarily acceptable, but the buyers should get advice and provide a choice before closing.

50. C. The law requires a written disclosure. The buyer's signature is desirable, but not required.

51. A. Undisclosed dual agency is the unfortunate result. This is why the addenda are to be signed at the time of the agency agreements to comply with company policy for in-company transactions.

52. C. The seller's agent does have legal duties to the buyer: fair and honest dealing and disclosure of material facts about the property. An agency relationship is implied with loyalty, fidelity, and full disclosure of all information.

53. B. The seller should say "no," since she has no knowledge at the present time. This is why buyers should understand that the seller disclosure is neither a warranty nor a guarantee. The seller may not know.

54. C. In Colorado, the licensee is relieved of disclosure of either fact by Colorado state law regarding stigmatized properties. Federal fair housing laws prohibit discussion of the AIDS-related death as a disability issue.

55. D. The subdivision developer's registration law requires registration with the commission for any property "divided into twenty or more interests intended solely for residential use and offered for sale, lease, or transfer."

56. B. Division of a single parcel into multiple parcels is a subdivision and must be done in compliance with local and state subdivision restrictions. The owner is not required to register with the real estate commission.

57. A. The Colorado Real Estate Recovery Fund will repay limited amounts to parties who are harmed by the actions of a licensee, cannot collect from the licensee, and have obtained a court judgment against the licensee. It provides no protection for the licensee or for investment losses.

58. D. A deed of trust using the public trustee is foreclosed through the public trustee's administrative process. A deed of trust using a private trustee must be foreclosed through the court like a mortgage.

59. A. The public trustee must hold a foreclosure sale 45 to 60 days following the lender's notice of default and request for sale. This time limit assures prompt action on deed of trust foreclosures through the public trustee. Legal notice is provided to the defaulting borrower who may cure the default until the day before the sale.

60. C. The borrow has a statutory period of redemption up to 75 days for non-agricultural property and up to 6 months for agricultural property.

61. B. The lender receives the proceeds up to the outstanding debt plus costs. Any excess will be returned to the borrower. Lenders receive the property only if they are the highest bidders at the auction.

62. A. The state engineer administers tributary water. The Colorado Ground Water Commission administers nontributary water in six defined water basins.

63. B. Small domestic wells are generally exempt from a requirement to obtain water rights but must still have a permit from the state engineer.

64. D. Water rights are real property. They may be sold separately and transferred by deed. Since they are not considered appurtenant, they must be specifically mentioned in a deed if the parties intend to include the water rights with a transfer of land.

65. B. Colorado law recognizes joint tenancy with right of survivorship, but not tenancy by the entirety or community property. Tenancy in severalty is ownership by a single individual.

66. B. The unequal division of ownership interests would invalidate the joint tenancy and create the default of tenancy in common. In order to create joint tenancy, the conveyance must have the unities of time, title, interest, and possession.

67. C. Colorado law requires a return of the deposit or accounting for the deposit in writing within one month, unless a specific lease agreement extends that time.

68. A. The Colorado Department of Revenue requires withholding of the lesser of 2 percent of the selling price or the entire net proceeds due to the seller at closing when the seller will be out of state after closing. There are several exemptions from this requirement.

69. B. Students are not a protected class under Colorado Fair Housing Act. Commercial space is covered under state law, so refusal to rent a studio for African American art would be a violation. The pool danger is a matter for the parents to decide, not the landlord.

70. C. However this syndication is organized, it must comply with securities regulations. Though probably exempt from federal registration requirements, the project must still comply with full disclosure rules. The broker will be a partner and must disclose his interest and any gains to the other owners.

71. A. The rental pool arrangement for income may qualify the offering as a security. The elements of a security do not appear to be present in the sale of mountain sites offered over the Internet, the condo project that includes residential and retail uses, or the speculative purchase of raw land by a doctor.

72. B. The buyer and seller are committing fraud. If any broker involved knows of the arrangement, the broker is also committing fraud and risks license discipline as well.

73. B. Every lease contains an implied warranty of quiet enjoyment only. The Colorado Supreme Court decided that leases do not contain an implied warranty of habitability. Tenants are responsible for determining if the property is satisfactory to their needs before signing a lease.

74. C. The Colorado Statute of Frauds requires any lease of real property for more than one year to be in writing. A month-to-month lease may be terminated with proper notice, so it may not last more than one year. However, it is always good practice for a lease to be in writing.

75. C. In an agency relationship, the seller may be liable for the acts of the broker within the scope of the agency. Disclosing this liability is a statutory duty.

76. B. All licensees have a statutory duty to disclose material facts about a property that are actually known to the broker. Facts about the seller or about the transaction in general must be disclosed only if material and failure to disclose would be fraud if disclosure is required by law.

77. C. All fixtures will be included unless excluded by the seller. The list helps to identify what fixtures are on the premises. A listed item that is not on the premises is not be included and does not need to be crossed out.

78. A. General practice uses a general warranty deed. Many situations, such as an estate sale, call for another type of deed and should be specified in both the listing and the sales contracts.

79. D. The listing should show all encumbrances known to the seller. The status of these encumbrances after a sale of the property is not relevant at the time of the listing.

80. D. The seller has the choice to provide the disclosure but is responsible to disclose hidden material defects in any case. Most offers from prospective buyers will call for the disclosure form leading to a negotiation on this point at a later time.

81. C. The protection is for a negotiated time after the listing expires, but it ends if the property is subsequently listed exclusively with another broker.

82. D. The seller may give permission for in-company transactions, in which case brokerage policy specifies a particular addendum for consistent use by all associates of the broker.

83. A. The forms are specific in allowing the seller and broker to divide the funds equally but limit the broker's share to no more than the commission would have been.

84. C. The listing contract forms are specific in requiring mediation in good faith before submitting the matter to arbitration or litigation.

85. A. The buyer can be an unrepresented "customer" after appropriate disclosure, can sign an agency representation agreement, or can hire the broker as a transaction-broker either in an exclusive arrangement, oral agreement, or by default.

86. D. The key to "reasonable efforts" is for the broker to match properties to the buyer's needs and show them, or attempt to show them, to the buyer.

87. C. While the buyer may direct the broker to seek payment from various sources, the buyer is ultimately responsible to assure that the broker is paid in full.

88. C. All compensation the buyer's broker receives must be disclosed. The retainer may be credited to other payments or not, as negotiated. Hourly fees may be in addition to other compensation if that is what the parties agree.

89. B. Exclusive-Right-to-Buy Contracts clearly state that the buyer is responsible for contacting local law enforcement officials if the possible presence of registered sex offenders is a concern.

90. B. Items likely to be leased, such as security systems, water softeners, smoke/fire detectors and satellite systems, are included only if the appropriate box is checked.

91. C. The form provides the first option by filling in a dollar amount and checking a box. The second option, seller reducing the price, must be written in after checking a different box. Since the contract provides the opportunity to specify a solution, the seller's innocent misstatement of the balance would not terminate the contract.

92. B. The entry for cash at closing amount completes the arithmetic for the sources of funds to equal the total purchase price. This amount is not intended to represent final figures, and it does not include closing costs or new loan fees.

93. C. If the buyer has not received a satisfactory commitment, the buyer may terminate by written notice to the seller, or the buyer may elect to continue with the contract but risks default and loss of the earnest money if the loan is not funded at closing.

94. D. Failure to specify at least one option is improper. One of the checked boxes will always apply. Either the appraisal provision is to be waived, or it will apply to a specific loan or to the buyer's evaluation of a cash purchase or loan assumption.

95. B. Some of the extended coverage applies to matters that a survey and physical inspection would reveal. The title company may call for a survey or improvement location certificate. The form provides for negotiating the responsibility to pay for the survey or ILC with the seller contributing up to a set amount (which may be zero) and the buyer responsible for any balance. The seller is responsible for additional premium.

96. D. Common interest communities are subject to a mandatory association assessment to support some common elements. Even single-family home developments often add this power to maintain common amenities such as greenbelts or recreational facilities.

97. A. If the buyers choose to terminate, they must provide written notice to the seller no later than the Off-Record Matters date. Termination is not automatic; it requires written notice of intent to terminate.

98. C. Colorado rules for this federal disclosure requirement provide that the contract is void unless proper disclosure is made prior to the parties signing the sales contract. The disclosure should be available at the property to assist cooperating brokers in complying with this requirement.

99. B. The form specifically relates to the seller's current actual knowledge.

100. C. The buyers are the sole judge of what conditions may cause them to terminate. If they list items for the seller to correct, the seller has until the Resolution Deadline to propose a satisfactory solution. One day following that deadline, the contract will terminate automatically unless the buyers withdraw the objections.

101. C. The buyer is responsible for obtaining the inspection and submitting any objections prior to the deadline. If the buyer does not file an objection, regardless of the reason for not filing, the inspection contingency is waived.

102. D. The contract calls for replacement with a unit of similar size, age, and quality or an equivalent credit at closing.

103. A. The walk-through is to verify that the condition is as agreed by contract. New items cannot be brought up after the Inspection Objection Deadline.

104. D. This legal phrase means that timing is important to the contract, and every date and deadline must be taken care of on or before that time.

105. A. Liquidated damages are defined as a predetermined sum that becomes the seller's sole and only remedy for default by the buyer. The seller may keep the earnest money but has no other options.

106. D. The contract states that these costs shall be awarded to the prevailing party. The award of fees to the broker is only in the special case of a dispute over earnest money that the broker interpleads with the court for settlement.

107. A. Nonbinding mediation is the only dispute resolution required by the contract. After 30 days, if mediation does not reach a voluntary settlement, either party may proceed to arbitration or litigation.

108. B. The contract language permits the parties to approve facsimile signatures and allows for either party to request original signatures at closing or earlier.

109. C. The contract form provides for notice to be effective when received by either the other party or the broker working with that party. If this form of notice is not satisfactory, the contract must be altered.

110. B. The seller may properly reject the offer but make a counteroffer by checking the box, initialing the form, and submitting a counterproposal form attached to the original offer. The seller may accept but must do so in writing and also notify the buyer in writing.

111. C. The brokers' signatures acknowledge receipt of the earnest money deposit and confirm their brokerage relationship to the party with whom they are working. Signing does not make the broker a party to the agreement. These signatures are after the legend that says END OF CONTRACT

112. C. Since a broker is not a party to the Contract to Buy and Sell, exculpatory provisions are out of place. If a broker needs some form of confirmation from the buyer or seller, the broker should prepare a separate disclosure for that purpose.

113. B. The standard forms assist brokers in complying with the Conway-Bogue decision that gives real estate licensees the limited right to practice law by completing standard and approved forms. The commission has authority only over licensees. That authority already includes discipline for improper or incompetent practice. The commission cannot control "all transactions" since many are done without brokers.

114. A. When the broker has an unmodified agency agreement with the seller, the buyer must be represented by another broker or receive a disclosure stating the buyer will have no working relationship with the broker. The alternative is that the seller agrees in advance to modify the agency through a Transaction-Broker Addendum or Dual Agency Addendum to the listing. Both the buyer and the seller must agree to the same brokerage relationship for an in-company transaction to be possible.

115. C. Colorado license law requires that whenever a broker has a working relationship with one party, that relationship must be disclosed to any other party to a transaction or potential transaction.

116. C. Rule F-11 specifies certain conditions for the use of the Licensee Buyout Addendum. Among those are the guaranteed buyout and a situation where a buyout is offered to facilitate other transactions. In both cases, the listing company continues marketing the property to the public pending the buyout. If the principal broker or listing associate wish to purchase for personal or investment use before the listing expires, they should resign the listing relationship and proceed as principal in the transaction.

117. A. The form is specific in providing that the brokerage company is responsible only if the broker signs the Licensee Buyout Addendum. If the broker wants the property for personal use, he or she must cancel the listing and simply submit a purchase offer as principal.

118. B. There is a specific form, Agreement to Amend/Extend Contract with Broker, for altering any terms of a listing or other contracts between the broker and a member of the public. When a specific form exists, brokers are required to use the approved form for that function.

119. C. The forms contain different provisions for assumption of the loan upon sale of the property. Three versions are approved: Strict Due on Sale, Qualified Assumption, and Freely Assumable upon Sale of the Property.

120. B. This special purpose promissory note allows a prospective buyer to present earnest money in the form of a note (promise to pay) when the cash may be tied up or difficult to access immediately. It must be presented and paid before closing to assure that it represents good funds at closing. From the seller's perspective, the sooner the note is due, the better.

121. C. The addendum is very specific in pointing out this major difference in the broker's duties. All of the other duties remain in a transaction-broker relationship.

122. B. The form of the earnest money must always be included in the Contract to Buy and Sell. In the case of a note, the due date is material information. The listing broker holds the note until honored but will not sue for payment. The seller has options if the note is not honored.

123. D. A statement in the heading of the form confirms that brokers set their own company commission plan.

124. C. An in-company transaction means that the broker represents, or is working with, both parties to a transaction. Both license law and the two brokerage relationship addenda to the Contract to Buy and Sell include this definition.

125. A. One broker (company) may not represent one party as agent and work with another as transaction-broker in the same transaction. The broker may represent the seller and work with buyers as customers, represent both as a dual agent or work with both the buyer and seller as a transaction-broker.

126. D. Only the current listing broker actually "earns" a commission. Listing brokers traditionally agree to split listing commissions with cooperating selling brokers.

127. C. This listing is technically with the brokerage entity (company); therefore, the form should reflect the name of the company. The associate will sign at the bottom on behalf of the company.

128. D. The "Other Sellers" provision of the listing contract specifically provides permission from the seller to list properties for other sellers during the term of this listing. The listing licensee may show the property to buyers but is not obligated to purchase the property if no one else does.

129. D. The addendum provides permission to change the relationship if the situation arises. There is no immediate change in the relationship. Dual agency continues the possibility of vicarious liability under both the listing and dual agency. Confidentiality is assured by contract during the listing and includes any dual agency situation.

130. D. The buyer engages the broker as his or her exclusive broker and agrees to work only through this broker for this purchase. The broker may still work with other buyers. Either agency or transaction-broker relationships are available for the buyer and broker.

131. C. Listing brokers traditionally offer to compensate cooperating buyer's agents. Payment of fee does not determine agency. The broker cannot "force" the seller to pay since this would only be a negotiation with the offer.

132. C. The contract makes the appropriate disclosure to the seller, but the licensee is required by law to disclose his or her relationship to any other party to the transaction. The licensee must disclose known material defects, but "unknown" defects would be impossible to disclose.

133. B. The approved Exclusive-Agency Listing Contract allows the seller to negotiate a sale and not pay the broker. Most brokers prefer the more common exclusive right-to-sell contract.

134. C. While the broker must be able to withdraw funds, other licensed or unlicensed people can be authorized to sign on this account. The escrow account must be maintained in the name of the licensed brokerage, federally insured, and regularly reconciled to guard against commingling.

135. A. Colorado practice and commission rules establish this preference. The parties can always agree on any other practice they specify.

136. D. The account journal lists the movements of all funds nin chronological order, while the ledgers separate the funds by beneficiary.

137. D. If the first half of the general property tax has been paid by February 28, the balance must be paid by June 15 to avoid a penalty. This schedule, established by state law, is critical to handling taxes in a closing early in the year.

138. D. The ultimate purpose of trust accounts is to segregate broker's funds from funds held for others. The number of such accounts may relate to simpler bookkeeping. Most escrow accounts are not interest bearing (at least for the broker).

139. D. Many title insurance companies have their own form, but in the absence of such a form the broker would use the approved Closing Instructions. This form separately "engages" (a legal process) the title company or other closing entity on behalf of the seller and buyer. The closing company is then legally responsible to the parties for its work. The broker remains fully responsible as well. The form is used to create that engagement at or before the time that title insurance is ordered. Title companies may use their own form under their attorney's advice because they will probably include disclaimers not included in the commission form. It is an "either/or" choice about which form to use.

140. B. The teller's check provides immediate funds when presented. None of the others (broker's check, any corporate check, or check from buyer) is considered by the bank to be immediately available.

141. A. If the buyer and seller are in a dispute over earnest money, the broker's options include awaiting a mutual agreement and instruction, or interpleading the money with the court to decide where it should go. The court may award the broker the expenses involved with interpleading the money.

142. C. The Loan Commitment Deadline provision gives the buyer the right to terminate if he or she cannot get a satisfactory loan commitment by the deadline. Termination is defined in the contract to include return of all money and things of value, so return of the earnest money is automatic and not subject to dispute by the seller.

143. B. The broker should receive the listing company commission in one check from the closing and deposit it in the operating account for distribution. It should not be left in the trust account after closing, as this would be commingling. The broker would not withhold independent contractor taxes and contributions.

144. C. The broker holds the note, but the broker is not a collection agent. If the note is not redeemed when due, the seller must decide on the appropriate action. The note must be redeemed far enough in advance of closing to assure good funds at closing.

145. C. No account is required until the broker actually must hold money belonging to others. Some brokers deposit funds directly with a title or escrow company and avoid opening trust accounts altogether.

146. B. State law authorizes a nonprofit affordable housing fund to collect the interest. Any other interest-bearing trust account must have a very specific agreement on the beneficiary of the interest. No party has an automatic claim to the interest.

147. C. Commission rules call for security deposits to be held in a separate trust account to prevent accidental commingling with operating expenses.

148. B. A multiple-client account is legal, but it could allow commingling by letting one owner's funds go below zero, which automatically uses another owner's money.

149. C. The Colorado Real Estate Commission may audit a broker's files at any time, without notice. This is a power granted to the commission to allow it to protect funds belonging to the public.

150. D. License law requires that the broker keep transaction records for a minimum of four years.

151. B. Rule E-5 requires the licensee who personally established the brokerage relationship to verify and sign this form for the party with whom the licensee has a relationship.

152. C. Commission rule specifies deposit into a trust account not later than one business day after the broker learns of acceptance of the offer.

153. D. If the check does not clear, the broker should notify the seller. The seller should choose whether to attempt to collect the earnest money or simply cancel the contract. The broker has no authority to make this choice.

154. B. The listing is an agreement between the seller and listing broker. No other party needs to retain a copy.

155. B. Credit union account insurance only covers members of the credit union and not all beneficiaries of the account. The commission position statement provides guidance that these accounts should not be used.

156. C. The purchase price benefits the seller's cash at the closing (credit) and causes the buyer to bring more cash to closing (debit).

157. A. On the settlement worksheet, credit the buyer and debit the broker.

158. B. The loan balance represents money the seller does not receive (debit) because it was not part of the equity in the property. The buyer receives a credit for this source of purchase funding.

159. B. Credit the buyer for the second deed of trust. Debit the seller, who accepts a promise to pay in place of cash at closing.

160. A. Line 6 proration is always 1 month's interest prorated to exact days in the month. $127,538 x .085 divided by 12 divided by 31 x 10 = $291.42.

161. A. By contract, the seller pays this cost, and the broker writes the check from the escrow account to the title company.

162. A. The abstractor charges for certifying to date. The warranty deed is entered after the sale. The buyer's attorney fees would be on a different line, and recording fees would not be paid to the abstractor.

163. C. Attorney fees to examine the title documents is normally the buyer's responsibility (debit) and a credit to the broker who then pays from the closing.

164. B. Recording the new deed benefits the buyer by providing constructive notice of his or her new interest; thus, debit the buyer.

165. A. This and most other charges connected with borrowing money would be charged to the buyer/borrower (debit) and a credit to the broker.

166. C. The charge for recording a release of deed of trust is a debit to the seller and a credit to the broker. The seller must clear the title of this former encumbrance. The broker will assure that the release is properly processed.

167. A. The documentary fee is one penny per \$100. \$245,900 divided by \$100 x \$.01 = \$24.59.

168. B. The buyer is normally responsible for this charge (Certificate of Taxes Due) with the broker writing a check at closing for the cost.

169. A. Taxes for the preceding year are entirely the seller's responsibility and were all delinquent on June 16 of this year. The tax plus penalties must be paid now. Debit the seller; credit the broker.

170. A. These taxes are not payable yet on February 23. By crediting the buyer the full amount, the buyer now has the option of either the single payment or two payment options for the payment of taxes. If the broker simply pays the taxes, this removes valuable options for the buyer. There should be a specific agreement that, contrary to the terms of the purchase agreement, the seller is not delivering the property free and clear of these taxes.

171. C. Either the new lender will insist on having the buyer place the full amount of these taxes in the tax impound account for the new lender to pay in April (debit seller, credit buyer), or the new lender will want the taxes paid through the closing (debit seller, credit broker). The broker must close based on the lender's method.

172. C. The seller owned for 253 days through September 10. \$3,685 divided by 365 x 253 = \$2,554.26 debit to the seller, \$2,554.26 credit to the buyer.

173. C. This year's taxes must be prorated between buyer and seller in every case unless the closing is on January 1, in which case the seller owns the property for zero days in this year.

174. B. If it is a loan assumption, a reserve (for taxes) still held by the lender will transfer to the buyer. Debit the buyer, credit the seller.

175. C. This amount will be withheld from the proceeds to "prime" the impound account to assure a sufficient balance to pay the taxes the following year.

176. A. Special assessments to be assumed by the buyer do not show up on the settlement. The presumption is that the buyer was aware of the improvements and the obligation, which were represented in the price offered for the property.

177. C. A new lender will not permit the special assessment to have priority over the new first loan and will pay off the special assessment from the loan proceeds. This will show as a single entry charging the seller for the payoff amount.

178. A. Personal property taxes are levied in the same manner as general property tax on real property, but they apply only to property used in business. If they apply, there is an annual tax bill, and a sale of the business, including the personal property, would include a proration of the personal property tax on that property.

179. C. Insurance contracts have specific named insured individuals and coverage selected by the policy owner. Transferring this contract to a new owner is difficult and unwise. The new owner should obtain new insurance.

180. D. Different ages of loans and property types have different premium payment methods. Each loan must be analyzed to determine the appropriate proration between buyer and seller.

181. B. Reserve accounts are also called "impound" accounts. The lender is collecting on a monthly basis to pay a future annual bill.

182. C. Either the buyer, the seller, or a combination of the two may pay loan discount points in most cases. Check the contract to determine the agreement between the parties.

183. C. Three discount points will raise the yield on a normal 30-year monthly payment loan by about 3/8 of 1 percent. In this case, the yield goes from 7 4/8 to 7 7/8, or 7.875.

184. B. Discount points are charged on the loan amount, not the sale price. $275,000 x .80 x .02 = $4,400. The lender will withhold the points from proceeds and the broker charges the seller who agreed to pay. Debit the seller.

185. C. Interest on a new loan is calculated on a per diem basis (divide by 365). $45,000 x .09 divided by 365 x 15 (buyer days in August) = $166.44 debit the buyer and credit the seller, who is the lender in this case. Note: the October 1 payment will include all of the interest for September, so only the remainder of August must be collected.

186. C. The contract contains check boxes to indicate which party agrees to pay for the survey.

187. C. Unpaid water bills can be a lien on the property. The broker must protect against such a lien by withholding seller funds to pay the final bill. Once the bill is paid, any excess can be returned to the seller.

188. C. Each party must pay his or her share of the bill (8 seller days and 83 buyer days), and the broker pays the entire past-due bill. Simply crediting the buyer with the seller's share would leave the possibility of a lien.

189. B. The bill is for 62 days ("to" May 15 does not include May 15). $47 divided by 62 x 55 = $41.69.

190. C. The seller has already collected the rent for unit A and owes the buyer the balance of the month. Offsetting that entry, the buyer will collect the entire rent for unit B and owes the seller for the seller's ownership period. Unit A: $475 divided by 30 x 24 = $380 seller owes buyer. Unit B: $525 divided by 30 x 6 = $105 buyer owes seller. Net = $275 seller owes buyer (debit seller, credit buyer).

191. B. This entry transfers the deposits to the new owner. The tenants should be informed that the new owner now holds their deposits.

192. A. The broker must close to the lender's assumption figures that indicate a payment due. When the seller's check arrives, the lender will refund the payment. The broker should alert the lender of this probability.

193. B. The broker's fee is normally shown on the settlement statement as debit the seller, credit the broker. The broker will clear this out of the escrow account by writing a check to the broker's operating account.

194. C. This amount is the amount of the check from the lender that is deposited into the closing escrow account. It is a single entry broker debit. The net loan proceeds plus all of the single entries allocated to the buyer and seller will exactly equal the gross loan amount credited to the buyer. Thus, the worksheet will be in balance.

195. C. The gross amount of the new loan is a buyer credit single entry. Later entries on the worksheet will charge the buyer for the closing costs that bring the net proceeds down.

196. D. Rule E-5 states that the selling licensee must confirm the figures and sign the Statement of Settlement. Other rules give the listing broker primary responsibility of the overall closing. These obligations are not removed by retaining a title insurance company or other closing company to do the actual closing calculations.

197. C. If the buyer agrees to the personal check, this will save the closing and make the calculations on the settlement worksheet accurate. The parties should also sign an informal memo that they have accepted this method of dealing with the improper allocation.

198. D. Since the problem is relatively minor, closing in escrow is a good alternative. All parties will sign the appropriate documents and entrust them to the title company or other closing entity. When the file is complete, the closing can be formalized.

199. B. You are responsible to be at the closing, but you may delegate your authority to another licensee who will sign the documents and assume joint liability for the accuracy of the buyer's closing figures.

200. B. The withholding required is the lesser of 2 percent of the selling price ($4,000) or the total cash proceeds ($4,500). In this case the 2 percent figure is smaller.